MW01152278

Dunning

FRANK THOMAS

FRANK THOMAS
Baseball's
BIG HURT

Stew Thornley

Lerner Publications Company • Minneapolis

Information for this book was obtained from the author's interview with Frank
Thomas and the following sources: *Advertising Age, Chicago Tribune, Current
Biography, Frank Thomas: The Big Hurt* by Ted Cox (Chicago:
Children's Press, 1994), *Sport, Sports Illustrated*, and *The Sporting News*.

This book is available in two editions:
Library binding by Lerner Publications Company
Soft cover by First Avenue Editions,
241 First Avenue North, Minneapolis, Minnesota 55401
International Standard Book Number: 0-8225-3651-X (lib. bdg.)
International Standard Book Number: 0-8225-9759-4 (pbk.)

LIBRARY OF CONGRESS CATALOGING-IN-PUBLICATION DATA

Thornley, Stew.
  Frank Thomas : baseball's big hitter / Stew Thornley
    p.   cm.
  Includes bibliographical references and index.
  Summary: A biography of the power-hitting baseball player, from
his childhood in Georgia through his college days at Auburn
University to his professional career with the Chicago White Sox.
  ISBN 0-8225-3651-X (hc). — ISBN 0-8225-9759-4 (pbk.)
  1. Thomas, Frank, 1968– —Juvenile literature. 2. baseball
players—United States—Biography—Juvenile literature. 3. Chicago
White Sox (Baseball team)—Juvenile literature. [1. Thomas, Frank,
1968–. 2. Baseball players. 3. Afro-Americans—Biography.]
I. Title.
GV865.T45T46   1997
796.357'092—dc21
[B]   96–51524

Manufactured in the United States of America
1 2 3 4 5 6 – JR – 02 01 00 99 98 97

Contents

Frank Thomas batting is a scary sight for pitchers.

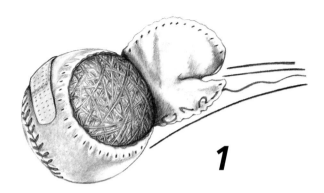

1

Big Hits from The Big Hurt

The Chicago White Sox were fighting for a playoff spot in September 1996. As usual, they were counting on their big first baseman, Frank Thomas, to get a big hit for them. The White Sox were in Boston to play the Red Sox, another team hoping to get into the playoffs. Fenway Park in Boston is known for its huge green leftfield fence. Thirty-seven feet high, the fence is known as the "Green Monster."

In the first inning, Frank took his place in the batter's box and looked out at Boston pitcher Tim Wakefield. Wakefield isn't like most pitchers, who throw fastballs and curveballs. Wakefield's main pitch is a knuckleball, a slow pitch that jumps around as it approaches the plate. It may look easy to hit, but it can jump in a different direction at the last second and drive a batter crazy. But Frank isn't just any batter. He can hit anything.

Frank's nickname is "The Big Hurt." He promotes a line of clothing that bears that name.

Wakefield's knuckleball floated up. Frank took a big swing. He hit the ball solidly and lifted a long drive down the leftfield line. The ball cleared the Green Monster and landed on the street beyond. The blast not only put the White Sox ahead, but it also gave Frank the most home runs in the history of the White Sox. The homer was his 215th, a team record. Frank's nickname around the league is "The Big Hurt" because of how he can put the hurt on a ball—and on opposing

pitchers. But Frank was more concerned about helping his team win than he was about setting records.
The White Sox would need more hits from him.

Chicago trailed, 3–1, in the third inning when
Frank came up for the second time. Once again,
Wakefield threw a knuckleball and, once again, Frank
went deep with it. He launched another shot over the
Monster—this one bouncing into a parking garage
across the street. Two batters later, teammate Danny
Tartabull connected for a home run. The game was
tied. "I guess it's going to be a good day," said Boston
first baseman Mo Vaughn as Frank rounded the bases
after his home run. Vaughn and Frank had played
against each other in college. Like Frank, Vaughn had
become a great slugger in the majors and had also hit
two home runs in this game.

But Frank wasn't done yet. He couldn't afford to
be. Boston scored a run in the bottom of the fourth
to go ahead again. Frank quickly took care of that in
the fifth inning. Wakefield got a strike on Frank and
then decided to try something different. Instead of
the usual knuckleball, Wakefield fired a fastball.
Frank wasn't fooled. He got around on the pitch and
sent a line drive toward left centerfield. The ball kept
rising and rising until it sailed over the high green
fence for Frank's third home run of the game. Even
though he was playing against their team, the Boston
fans gave Frank a standing ovation.

Frank ties the game against the Red Sox with this blast, his third home run of the game.

When Frank came to the plate in the seventh inning, the White Sox had fallen behind again. This time, though, the Red Sox wouldn't give Frank a chance to take away their lead with another home run. They walked Frank on purpose. The strategy didn't pay off, however. Frank came around to score as part of a three-run rally.

But this was one of those days when all that Frank did was not enough. Despite his three home runs and four runs scored, the White Sox ended up losing the game. It was the first three-homer game of Frank's career, something he should have been excited about. Instead, he sat dejectedly in the locker room after the game. "The three homers were nice because I've never done it in my career," he said, "but this was a tough loss."

While Frank can send pitches a long way, as he did in this game, he doesn't concentrate on hitting home runs. Standing 6-foot-5 and weighing more than 250 pounds, he looks like a home-run hitter. But he goes for a balanced approach at the plate. He can hit the ball hard to all parts of the field. He gets a lot of hits of all types, not just home runs.

"I'm not trying to be a bad boy when I go up to bat," Frank claims. "I'm not taking a home-run cut every time. I don't even have a home-run trot. This is my physical appearance. I worked very hard for it. But I don't play it up."

Frank doesn't hit home runs every day. No one does. But Frank does get on base in most games. It may not be a home run or even a single that gets him on base. Frank is also valuable because of his ability to draw walks. Sometimes Frank walks because pitchers are afraid to throw him anything too good to hit. But Frank also has a remarkable eye at the plate. He rarely swings at anything outside the strike zone. Since he came to the majors in 1990, Frank has never gone more than two games without getting a hit or drawing a walk.

His ability to get on base means he scores large numbers of runs in addition to getting a lot of **runs batted in** (RBIs) when he does hit the ball. On top of that, he runs extremely well for a big man and is a threat on the base paths.

But what strikes terror into pitchers isn't Frank's speed or his knack for drawing walks. When Frank swings and connects, it can be a scary experience for anyone in the path of the ball. "I wish they'd let us put on a mask and shin guards," veteran hurler Dennis Martinez says about pitching when Frank is batting. "Pitchers shouldn't be left alone with him out there."

Sometimes, after Frank hits the ball, he just knows it's out of the park.

For his high school senior picture, Frank wore a suit and tie. But most of the time, he was wearing a Columbus High School sports uniform.

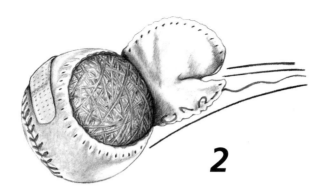

2

Winning and Losing

Frank was the fifth child in his family. He was born in Columbus, Georgia, on May 27, 1968. His mother, Charlie Mae, worked in a textile factory in Columbus. His father, Frank Senior, was a bail bond agent. He also served as a deacon in the local Baptist church.

Frank Sr. had been a pretty good athlete in his day, on the sandlots of Columbus. He wasn't good enough to make a living at sports, though, and had to work at other jobs to support his family. He hoped for better things for his children, especially his youngest son.

For a long time, Frank was the baby of his family. Then, in 1975, Frank Sr. and Charlie Mae had another child, a daughter named Pamela. Even though Pamela was seven years younger than Frank, the two became each other's favorite person.

When he wasn't playing with his little sister, Frank was usually playing some kind of sport—football, baseball, or basketball. "Frank did so well in all sports," said his father. "I never had to worry about him. If he wasn't home, I knew he was at the Boys Club or the playground, somewhere with a ball in his hands. He had a gift and, most important, was willing to learn."

One of the things Frank was learning was to avoid swinging at bad pitches. Even then, he was developing the sharp batting eye that would become his trademark in the major leagues. "Kids would throw the ball behind him, over the backstop, all over the place," said his dad. "They'd do anything to avoid pitching to him."

Frank could do much more than hit. In baseball, he had a strong throwing arm. He could sometimes throw out runners at first base from his position in centerfield. As a tight end in football, he put crunching blocks on older, but not necessarily bigger, defensive players. "I hung out with my older brother and his friends," Frank says, "and I got pushed around a lot until I started pushing back."

Chester Murray, Frank's coach in Pop Warner football, says he knew Frank would become a professional athlete someday. "I don't know in what sport," said Murray. "But he will be a professional athlete."

On the athletic fields, Frank was learning to win. Off the fields, though, he was learning about loss.

In 1977, Pamela became sick. Her illness was diagnosed as leukemia, a form of cancer. She spent much of her time at Egleston Children's Hospital in Atlanta, far away from Columbus. One weekend, Pamela came home. The cancer treatments had robbed her of her hair, but she still had a smile for her big brother.

Frank was nine. He struggled to understand what was happening to his sister. Then, on Thanksgiving Day, Pamela died. She was just two and a half years old.

Not long after her death, Frank said to his father, "Dad, maybe someday I'll be able to do something about it." He knew he could never bring Pamela back, but he hoped he might someday be able to help find a cure for the disease that had killed her. At 10, Frank knew there were many ways he could do this. He could become a doctor or a scientist. But he also knew how much impact sports stars have. The money they make and the influence they have can make a difference in many areas, in and out of the sports world. Frank became more determined than ever to become a professional athlete and to use his influence in a way that would help others. From that point on, Frank dedicated himself to becoming a major league baseball player in Pamela's honor.

When Frank got to high school, his baseball heroes were Dave Parker and Dave Winfield. Both were large men—as Frank Sr. was and Frank Jr. was becoming—who could hit for both power and a high **batting average.** Frank also played basketball and football at Columbus High School. His favorite pro football player was Walter Payton, a running back with the Chicago Bears. But Frank played tight end for Columbus High. In his senior year, he caught 30 passes for more than 400 yards. He also kicked extra points following touchdowns and didn't miss a single one all year.

On the baseball diamond, Frank put up impressive numbers. Columbus won the state high school championship in 1984, when Frank was a sophomore. Two years later, Columbus finished second in the state tournament. Frank had a big season, hitting .450 with 13 home runs and 52 RBIs in just 30 games.

Frank played tight end and first base for the Blue Devils.

Frank was thinking about attending Auburn University in Auburn, Alabama, not far from Columbus. He would receive a scholarship to play football, not baseball, for the Auburn Tigers.

But then Frank had other thoughts. A number of major league baseball teams' scouts had noticed Frank's high school performance. Each year, major league baseball teams draft players who have graduated from high school or who are playing in college. The teams take turns choosing players and offering them money to play baseball. Usually the players are sent to minor league teams to improve before they play with the major league teams.

Frank expected to be drafted. He made up his mind that he was going to sign a professional baseball contract. He'd start out in the minor leagues and work his way up to the majors.

On the day of the baseball draft, Frank waited anxiously for a team to draft him. But the phone in the Thomas home never rang. Not one of the 26 major league baseball teams drafted Frank.

Many teams later claimed they hadn't drafted Frank because they thought he would be going to college to play football. But Frank said, "If a team had drafted me, I would have signed with them on the spot. That was my dream—to play baseball."

Frank would play baseball, but not as a professional. Frank would be a college student.

Football coach Pat Dye persuaded Frank to attend Auburn.

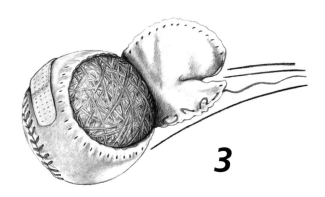

3

Auburn All Star

Auburn University recruited Frank to play football. But football coach Pat Dye told Frank he could also play on the Tigers' baseball team. This meant that Frank would have to miss the early football practices held each spring.

Dye was used to this type of situation. He had allowed a similar arrangement with another outstanding player who had just finished his college career. Bo Jackson was, like Frank, a multitalented athlete who played both football and baseball for Auburn. Missing spring football practice to play baseball hadn't hurt Jackson. In his senior year, he won the Heisman Trophy as the top college football player in the country. Jackson eventually played both baseball and football professionally.

The Auburn football team was so good in 1986 that Frank couldn't crack the starting lineup. He did get into all of the team's games, though. As a tight end, Frank spent more time blocking than catching passes, but he still contributed to the team's success. Auburn played in the Citrus Bowl and finished the season ranked sixth in the nation.

Frank had more chances to shine on the baseball diamond. In just his second game as a freshman, he had four hits—including a **grand slam** and a three-run homer—in a 23–2 rout of the University of Alabama at Birmingham.

Baseball coach Hal Baird knew he had a special player on his team. "Frank was a polished player when he came to us, and he had a very analytical approach to the game for a high school kid," said Baird. "From the first couple of days I saw him, I thought he was the best I ever saw."

Frank hit 21 home runs in his first season to set an Auburn record. He set another school record by drawing 73 walks in just 59 games and also had a batting average of .359. He was named to *Baseball America's* Freshman All-America team. Frank had the chance to play against other top college players who went on to become stars in the major leagues. One such player, Joey Belle (who later became known as Albert Belle), played for Louisiana State. Auburn advanced to the regional playoffs in 1987 and played Seton Hall, a team that featured Craig Biggio and Mo Vaughn.

In college, Frank decided to concentrate on baseball.

After the baseball season, Frank began preparing for another season of football. He wanted to play more, so he worked hard on improving his strength and quickness. But on the first day of practice in the fall of 1987, Frank strained some ligaments in his knee. He also developed bone spurs in his ankle. He decided to give up football and concentrate on baseball. He gave up his football scholarship and was able to get a baseball scholarship.

Getting hurt in practice made Frank think about how common injuries are to football players. Frank said he had seen "too many of my friends in football, guys with unbelievable talent, go down with injuries. One day, you might get torn ligaments that you could never rebuild. Or a broken neck—I saw a couple of unbelievable broken necks. That's why I switched after one season."

Frank knew that his talent was really in baseball, not football. "In baseball, I could dominate," said Frank. "I still had a lot of work to do in football. I loved football, but I really loved baseball. I played college football because it was my only choice. But I was grateful for a football scholarship. And, looking back, it was a blessing it worked out that way."

Frank and Bo Jackson were often compared to each other because they both played baseball and football at Auburn. But Hal Baird, who coached both of them on the baseball team, saw a difference between the two. "Bo was always a football and baseball player," said Baird. "Frank, I believe, was a baseball player who also played football. Frank understood the art of hitting better than any player I've seen."

Bo Jackson was an outstanding football and baseball player at Auburn University before Frank arrived.

Bo Jackson left Auburn in the spring of 1986. He just missed playing baseball with Frank, who entered Auburn in the fall of 1986.

With football behind him, Frank was able to concentrate solely on baseball in 1988, his sophomore season. "[Football] made me a man," he later said. "I had always thought I was working hard. But then I learned what hard work really means." Frank got off to a quick start in his sophomore season. He hit a home run in his first **at bat.** Frank's best game of the season was against Jacksonville State when he hit a pair of three-run homers and had eight RBIs.

Frank led his team in eight different offensive categories and was the conference batting champion with a .385 average. He was becoming a legend in the Southeastern Conference with fans and opposing players alike. Players from other teams often stopped their pregame warmup exercises just so they could watch Frank take batting practice. At first, Frank was embarrassed by this kind of attention but he quickly became used to it.

Frank had seen a lot of bad pitches during his Little League and high school days, and he had drawn plenty of walks. He claims, however, that he never really learned to be patient while batting until he went to Auburn.

Steve Renfro, an Auburn assistant baseball coach, often talked to Frank about looking for a good pitch to hit. "Pitchers aren't going to just give you pitches on a silver platter," Renfro told him. "You have to make them throw you something good, something you want to hit. You have to be patient. A lot of good hitters at your level can swing a bat, but the ones who make an impact in the major leagues are the ones who make the pitcher throw them their pitch."

This meant that Frank had to do more than just not swing at pitches outside the strike zone. Frank also had to learn to be selective about the strikes at which he would swing. If he could get ahead in the **count** (meaning that he had more balls than strikes on him), he would have an advantage over the pitcher. Even if the next pitch was a strike, Frank wouldn't have to swing unless he liked the pitch.

Frank learned that the formula for hitting success was this: to get ahead in the count by being selective and then be just as selective about even the good pitches. "A good at bat for me is to take the count full [three balls and two strikes] and then get the pitch that I want," he says.

Frank learned his lesson well while playing college baseball. "You can only hit what a pitcher gives you," he said. "If there's a pitch I can't sting like I want to, I leave it alone. Being patient is something that's easy to say, hard to do. But if you can do it, eventually the pitcher has to come to you."

At the end of the college season, Frank became a member of the U.S. National Team. Playing with some of the top college players from across the country, Frank held his own. He had a .313 batting average and looked forward to being able to play in the Olympics in Seoul, South Korea. But coach Mark Marquess cut Frank from the team before the Olympics. Marquess took Tino Martinez of Tampa College as the first baseman instead of Frank. Frank was shocked and hurt. He felt the way he had when he hadn't been drafted out of high school. "I couldn't believe it," Frank said.

Some people respond to rejection by moping. Others are determined to show those who rejected them that they made a mistake. That is what Frank did.

In 1989, Frank did it all. He helped the Tigers win the Southeastern Conference Tournament. Frank also led the conference with a .403 batting average and 83 runs batted in. His 19 home runs gave him 49 for his college career, setting an Auburn record. The conference named Frank as its Most Valuable Player. He was also selected to *The Sporting News* All-America Team.

Auburn baseball coach Hal Baird encouraged Frank to pursue a career in professional baseball.

Frank had just finished his junior season and could play one more year of college baseball. But this time, the professional teams weren't going to let him get away. The Chicago White Sox selected Frank in the first round of the baseball draft. He was the seventh player picked overall. He left Auburn to pursue his professional career before he earned his college degree.

Auburn coach Hal Baird knew that he would miss having Frank on his team, but he wished him well. "We loved him," Baird said. "He was fun to be around—always smiling, always bright-eyed. Frank is the greatest player we've ever had."

Frank got, on average, a hit a game while he played for
the Class A Birmingham Barons in 1990.

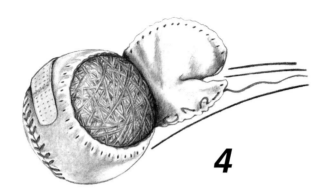

4

Making the Grade

Major league teams have "farm systems" to develop their young players. A farm system consists of minor league teams. These teams play at different levels. The lowest level is a rookie league for players who have just signed a professional contract. The levels move up to Class A, Class AA, and Class AAA. Class AAA is the highest level in the minors. If a player can survive the competition at these different levels, he may be able to play in the major leagues.

In 1989, the Chicago White Sox had two minor league teams in Sarasota, Florida. One was a rookie-level team in the Gulf Coast League. The other team was a Class A team in the Florida State League. After the White Sox drafted Frank, they assigned him to the Sarasota rookie team. Frank hit well, compiling a batting average of .365. After only 17 games, Frank was promoted to the Class A team in Sarasota. He didn't do quite as well there, but he still hit .277 with four home runs in 55 games. Overall, Frank had made a good start in professional baseball.

The White Sox organization is known for how hard it works its prospects. The young players have to take extra hitting and fielding practice before games, in addition to lifting weights. For Frank, the hard work was no problem. "It's a little tough, but I think what they are doing is working on your mental toughness as well," Frank said. "They want to push you to the limits, but I was used to that when I was playing football, so it's not that big of a change."

Frank went to spring training with the White Sox in 1990 and hit well. He had a .500 batting average in 12 exhibition games. White Sox manager Jeff Torborg thought Frank was ready for the major leagues. General manager Larry Himes was also tempted to keep Frank on the major league squad. But Himes had seen what had happened to some young players who were rushed along too quickly. If they advanced to a level they weren't ready for, they didn't play well and lost confidence. Sometimes a promising career was ruined. Himes didn't want this to happen with Frank. In the end, Himes went with his original plan to give Frank more time in the minor leagues.

Frank was one of the last players cut from the major league roster in spring training. Coming so close left him disappointed. "I dominated that spring," Frank said. "They didn't know how to handle that. They thought it was just a flash or that I was in a little groove. But that was me."

Frank started the 1990 season with the Class AA Birmingham Barons in the Southern League. On his way from Sarasota to Birmingham, Frank stopped in Columbus to visit his parents. Frank Sr. remembered how disappointed his son was at having to go back to the minors. "Those were the most down days in my boy's life: The day we lost my baby girl, the day nobody drafted him, and the day he didn't get to stay up," said Frank's dad.

But the previous setbacks seemed to have given Frank a renewed sense of purpose. This disappointment was no exception. "He was hurt," said Frank Sr., "but he was dedicated to working hard and being ready."

Frank's manager at Birmingham, Ken Berry, was happy to have such a great player. "He's having to make some adjustments, and he's got some work to do," Berry said of Frank. "It's a learning process for him, and he's got more to learn."

Meanwhile, Frank was determined to make his stay in Birmingham a short one. "Whenever they tell me," he said, referring to a call to the majors, "I'll be ready." But the call didn't come right away, even though Frank was tearing up Southern League pitching.

In June, Frank hit a mammoth home run at Engel Field in Chattanooga, Tennessee. Old-timers claimed that the only homer ever hit farther at Engel Field was one hit in 1957 by Harmon Killebrew, another powerful slugger.

The next month, Frank hit so well that he was named Southern League Player of the Month. Frank couldn't understand why he was still in the minor leagues. "I was stepping on the gas as much as possible," Frank said, "going night after night, hitting home run after home run, and wondering why the White Sox couldn't use me."

It wasn't that the White Sox hadn't noticed Frank. "Our awareness of Thomas's exploits was incredible," said Danny Evans, the White Sox director of baseball administration. "It got to the point where nobody ever used his last name. Every morning our people would ask, 'What did Frank do last night?'"

The White Sox finally called Frank up to the major league team on Thursday, August 2. Frank got to Milwaukee just in time for the beginning of a **twi-night doubleheader** against the Brewers. Frank didn't get a hit in his first three at bats. When he came to bat in the ninth inning, the game was tied. Ivan Calderon was on third base for the White Sox. Frank hit a soft **chopper** down the third-base line. Milwaukee third baseman Gary Sheffield scooped it up and threw home, trying to get Calderon. His throw was too late. The White Sox won the game, 4–3. Frank wasn't given a hit on the play—the official scorer ruled the play a **fielder's choice**—but he had driven in the winning run in his first major league game.

The next night, Frank got his first hit, and it was a big one. Milwaukee led Chicago, 1–0, in the seventh inning. With two runners on base, Frank connected for a triple to drive in both runs and put the White Sox ahead to stay.

The White Sox were in second place in the American League West Division when Frank joined them.

Frank tags Cleveland's Alex Cole, who was diving back to first base, in an attempted pickoff play during the 1990 season. Frank played in 60 games his first year.

They trailed the Oakland Athletics by four games. "We immediately pushed him into the heat of a pennant race," said Jeff Torborg. "He responded right away."

Frank was a welcome addition to the White Sox and quickly impressed his teammates. The team's star relief pitcher, Bobby Thigpen, said, "He has a lot of confidence. He's on the quiet side and doesn't say much. Off the field, he's not cocky or aggressive. He's the kind of guy everyone's pulling for."

The White Sox never did catch the first-place Athletics, but Frank had an outstanding year. Even though he had left the Barons with a month remaining in the Southern League schedule, Frank was named Minor League Player of the Year by *Baseball America*. For the White Sox, Frank hit .330 and smacked seven home runs. He drew 156 walks in 1990 (at Birmingham and Chicago), more than any other professional baseball player.

Over the winter, Frank went to Los Angeles to work on his hitting with Eric Davis and Darryl Strawberry, a couple of established major leaguers. Davis described Frank's hitting as, "Awesome. Totally." By the next spring, Frank was ready for his first full year in the major leagues.

Frank's 1991 season started off well, and not just on the baseball field. Frank met a young woman during spring training. After an exhibition game, Frank and his teammate Melido Perez stopped at a restaurant.

Inside, Frank bumped into a woman named Elise Silver, who was from Rochester, New York. Elise was in Florida to watch some spring training games. She knew baseball well. Her family had been involved with the Rochester Red Wings, a minor league team in the International League. The Red Wings' ballpark at that time, Silver Stadium, had been named after Elise's uncle, Morrie Silver.

Frank and Elise hit it off right away. They began dating. Within a year, they were married. "People might say there would be some cultural differences," said Elise, referring to the fact that she is white and Jewish and Frank is black and Christian. "But when you come from two loving families, it's pretty easy. Besides, we had baseball in common."

Because Frank had spent two months with the White Sox in 1990, he was not classified as a rookie in 1991. That was all that kept him from being named the American League Rookie of the Year. He hit 32 home runs, two of the biggest coming in a seven-game stretch in August. On the first Sunday in August, the White Sox were in second place, three games behind the Minnesota Twins. Frank broke up a scoreless game against Baltimore with a home run in the sixth inning. The White Sox went on to win, 1–0. A week later, Frank hit a two-run homer in the top of the first inning of a game at Baltimore. That was all White Sox lefthander Wilson Alvarez would need to win his first major league start. Alvarez pitched a no-hitter against the Orioles. Thanks to Alvarez and Frank, the White Sox completed a seven-game winning streak and pulled to within a game of the Twins in the standings.

That was as close as the White Sox could come in 1991. They faded after their winning streak although Frank continued his hot hitting. Frank was named American League Player of the Month in August. But he injured his wrist and had to miss a few games in September. The injury limited Frank's effectiveness during the final month of the season. Even so, he finished third in the balloting for American League Most Valuable Player.

The White Sox hoped to do better in 1992. Unfortunately, they ended up taking a step backward. Under new manager Gene Lamont, the White Sox finished in third place. Frank was as consistent as ever, though. Twice during the year he was named Player of the Week in the American League. In September, he was honored as Player of the Month. Although his home run total dropped to 24, he achieved a career high with 115 runs batted in.

Despite his great season, Frank wasn't named to the American League All-Star team in July. But something else happened to take his mind off that disappointment. On the day of the All-Star Game, Elise gave birth to a son, Sterling, the couple's first child.

Frank hit 24 home runs in 1992.

Because Frank didn't play in the game, he was able to be with Elise when Sterling was born.

   The White Sox had been frustrated in their title hopes during the previous few years. But with Frank Thomas on their team, they knew it was only a matter of time until they finished first.

By being picky about which pitches he swung at, Frank
cut down on the number of times he struck out.

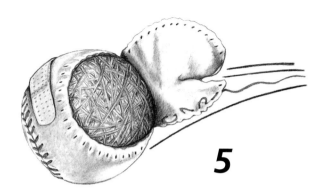

5

Doing It His Way

Fans quickly became accustomed to watching Frank hit home runs. But what set Frank apart from other power hitters was his discipline at the plate. He struck out 112 times in 1991, his first full year. Within two years, he had cut that total in half and was racking up nearly as many homers as strikeouts.

"The thing that impresses me about him is that he has such an intelligent approach to hitting for being so young," said David Cone, one of the top pitchers in the game. "It's tough to get him to chase bad pitches." Walt Hriniak, who was the White Sox batting coach when Frank joined the team, agrees. "If you could chisel out a hitter who swings only at what he can hit, it's Frank," said Hriniak.

But some people were suggesting that Frank should be less selective and chase a bad pitch once in a while. They said he should be more willing to swing

41

and less willing to draw a walk when the White Sox had runners in **scoring position.**

Hriniak had heard this type of criticism before. "Someone once said to me, 'If there's anything negative about Frank, it's that he's too selective,' " said Hriniak. "My response was, 'They said the same thing about Ted Williams.' " Ted Williams played for the Boston Red Sox from 1939 to 1960. He is often regarded as one of the two greatest hitters (Babe Ruth being the other) in the history of baseball. In 1941, Williams had a batting average of .406. That means he had more than 4 hits for every 10 at bats. Since 1941, no major league hitter has hit above .400 in a full season of play. Williams also connected for 521 career home runs, one of the top totals in this category, even though he missed several seasons while serving in the armed forces during World War II and the Korean War. To be compared with Ted Williams was quite an honor for Frank.

Frank works on his disciplined approach at all times, even in batting practice. While other players will take their cuts at all types of pitches in the practice cage, Frank is selective even there. He won't swing until he sees a pitch he can drive.

Of course, there's more than just his sharp eye that allows him to draw walks. Frank is such a good hitter that pitchers are often afraid to throw strikes to him. They do not like putting him on base by walking him.

Ted Williams played for the Boston Red Sox. He was one of the best hitters in the history of the game.

They'd rather try to get him out. But pitchers know Frank can do a lot of damage if they give him anything good to hit. Catchers understand that. "Walk Frank Thomas?" catcher Pat Borders once asked. "I've got no problem with that."

Former Yankees manager Buck Showalter said he would consider intentionally walking Thomas with the bases loaded, depending on the situation. Showalter never actually did that, but White Sox announcer Ken Harrelson says he expects to someday see a manager order an intentional walk to Frank, even with the bases loaded. "When that happens," Harrelson adds, "I'll stand up and applaud him for his intelligence."

Besides his disciplined manner at the plate, Frank is a real student of the game. He watches opposing pitchers closely. "I'll sit on the bench, and I'll watch a pitcher for the entire nine innings," he says. "I'll watch all his tendencies. I'll try to know everything I can about how he delivers a baseball." Frank even pays attention to the warmup pitches the pitchers throw between innings. With this kind of preparation, when it's his turn at bat, he's ready.

Frank was born with great ability, but he doesn't rely on his natural gifts. He works hard to get the most out of his talent. "I'm more of a blue-collar player, a grinder," he says of himself. "I've had to work for everything I've done. I sit there and watch myself on highlights and see that I don't do it as nice and fluid and sweet as some of the other players. And I'm proud of that."

Frank is one of the highest paid players in baseball, but he says the money isn't what motivates him. When asked what does, Frank replies, "Stats." Every day, he checks his batting statistics and sees how they compare to the other top hitters in the American

League. His teammates good-naturedly tease him by calling him the "Stat King."

Of all the statistics that are used to measure a hitter's performance, runs batted in are the most important to Frank because, he says, "They tell you how much you mean to your team."

A lot of players excel in one area. Some have high batting averages but few home runs. Others have great power but don't get on base that much. Frank likes to have good statistics in all categories. "Not many guys in this game have ever been able to hit for average, for power, and drive in runs," says Frank. "I like to combine all those things. I want to be one of those guys who make people say, 'Some of the things he did, I don't think can ever be done again.' "

Just so his head doesn't get too big, Frank keeps his ego under control. The letters D. B. T. H. are taped above his locker. The letters stand for his motto, "Don't Believe the Hype." Frank means that even with everything written about how great he is, he doesn't want to make a big deal out of it.

Even so, those around him know he is a great player. Julio Franco, once a teammate of Frank's, said, "Playing with Frank is like being part of history." White Sox announcer Ken Harrelson, who has watched a lot of great players, adds, "In another 30 years, we may be talking about Frank Thomas in the same way we now talk about Ted Williams."

Frank and Bo Jackson, right, never played together at Auburn, but they got the chance to be teammates on the White Sox in 1993.

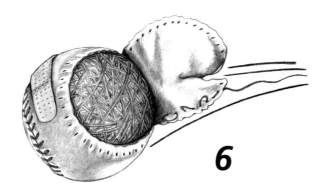

6

Breaking Through

Everything came together for Frank and the White Sox in 1993. One of the players who helped the White Sox try for a division crown was Bo Jackson. After leaving Auburn University the year before Frank started there, Jackson played both football and baseball professionally. His two-sport days ended when he suffered a serious hip injury on the football field in 1990. The injury also interrupted his baseball career because he had to have the hip replaced. With an artificial hip, Jackson returned to baseball in 1993.

The star of the 1993 White Sox team was clearly Frank Thomas. He set a White Sox record by hitting 41 home runs. Fifteen homers came in the first inning—which helped the White Sox get off to a good start in those games. "I call them my school bells," Frank said of his first-inning blasts. "It means the offense is in session."

Frank also took pride in his defense in 1993. He had never been regarded as a great fielder at first base. During the off-season, he worked hard on his fielding, spending a lot of time fielding ground balls. "My favorite moment this year was a play I made at first," Frank said. "I dove to my right, then threw home to get the runner. I don't think I could have made that play before this year."

Power, not defense, is Frank's strength. He has worked hard to improve his fielding.

Although that was Frank's favorite moment of the 1993 season, the White Sox fans' favorite came in an August game against the Kansas City Royals, who were challenging Chicago for first place. The Royals held a 4–2 lead late in the game and looked as if they would soon creep even nearer to the White Sox in the standings.

But Kansas City still had to get by Frank. A thick fog hung over Chicago's Comiskey Park as the Sox came to bat in the last of the eighth. Chicago started to rally. One run was in and the tying run was at second base when Frank stepped into the batter's box. Royals reliever Jeff Montgomery didn't want to give Frank anything good to hit and missed the strike zone with his first pitch. Montgomery's next pitch was over the plate and Frank made contact.

He drove the pitch toward deep leftfield. Fans in the stadium lost sight of the ball as it quickly disappeared into the fog. Even so, they let out a roar because they knew it was headed out of the ballpark.

Fireworks shot upward from behind the outfield fence as Frank circled the bases with a two-run homer. That hit was the difference in the game, which the White Sox won, 5–4. Chicago stayed in first place the rest of the season and won the division championship. "I hate to hang so much on one game, but that's as good as it gets," said manager Gene Lamont of the White Sox's dramatic victory that August night.

Frank's teammates congratulate him after he hit a two-run homer to beat Kansas City.

After finishing first in their division, the White Sox faced the Toronto Blue Jays in the league playoffs. The winner of this series would advance to the World Series. Toronto pitchers did what they could to keep Frank from hurting them in the series. In the first game, which Chicago lost, Frank walked four times. He singled in his only other trip to the plate.

That was a pattern for the entire series. The Toronto pitchers decided they would rather walk Frank than let him beat them with his bat. It turned out to be an effective strategy. Frank walked 10 times in six games, but his teammates weren't able to drive him in to score very often. Toronto beat Chicago, four games to two.

Despite this home run by Frank, Toronto defeated the White Sox in the 1993 American League playoffs.

With their season finished, the White Sox hoped their slugger would be recognized for his efforts. Frank was one of the top contenders for the American League Most Valuable Player award. But Frank remembered past disappointments. He did not dare to hope too much. But when the results were in, Frank had not only won the award, he had received all 28 first-place votes.

Frank, with his wife Elise holding their son Sterling, was happy to be the 1993 American League MVP.

Michael Jordan joined the White Sox organization in 1994, but he and Frank never got to play together.

Frank savored the honor but let his fans know he wouldn't let up. "You're not going to see a decline in my play," he said. "I'm still learning the game, and I'm still learning hitting."

Spring training was different for the White Sox in 1994. One of the players in camp was Michael Jordan, one of the greatest basketball players in history. Jordan had announced his retirement from the Chicago Bulls the previous fall, then said he wanted to play baseball. Many people criticized Jordan for what he was trying, but Frank supported him. "I want a player on my team who's not afraid of the big game, who loves the pressure," Frank said of Jordan. Jordan never did play in the majors with the White Sox and eventually returned to basketball.

Frank came back even stronger in 1994. He had 32 home runs by the All-Star break. Twice—in May and July—he was named American League Player of the Month. "Even though I was MVP in 1993, I think 1994 was a breakthrough year for me," Frank said. He felt he played even better in 1994 than he had the year before.

For the second straight year, Frank was voted the American League Most Valuable Player. There was only one thing wrong. The baseball players went on strike. The season came to an early halt in mid-August.

Frank had put up great numbers even though nearly a third of the season had been wiped out by the strike. The strike may also have cost the White Sox the chance to get to the World Series since they were leading their division when the season ended.

The strike did give Frank the opportunity to spend more time with his family, which had grown to four. Frank and Elise had a daughter, Sloan, in the spring of 1994.

Having children didn't mean that Frank forgot about his younger sister. When Pamela died of leukemia in 1977, Frank had hoped to one day be in a position to do something about the disease. As a major league star, he was. He established the Frank Thomas Charitable Foundation, which helps children and others in need. One of the organizations it benefits is the Leukemia Society of America.

Fans who want Frank's autograph must pay a dollar. The money goes to fight leukemia.

For every autograph Frank signs, even for his teammates, he asks for a dollar. Frank matches that dollar with one of his own and contributes the money to the Leukemia Society, in Pamela's memory.

Frank is grateful his own children are healthy. He doesn't need to be reminded that others aren't always as lucky. Frank's older sister, Mary, also knows that. Mary's son, Geoffrey, has sickle-cell anemia, a disease that primarily afflicts African Americans.

Frank cares about more young people than just those in his family. He's part of major league baseball's "Stay in School" program. He visits high schools in the Chicago area, helping students to understand the importance of a good education.

As if baseball, family, and other activities weren't enough to fill his schedule, Frank has also tried acting a couple of times. He had a small role in *Mr. Baseball*, a movie starring Tom Selleck, and also appeared in an episode of the television show, *Married . . . With Children*.

Sterling helps his dad answer reporters' questions after Frank was named MVP for a second time, in 1994.

Cleveland's Carlos Baerga high-fives Frank after Frank hit a two-run homer in the 1995 All-Star Game.

By the time the 1995 season opened, Frank was more than happy to get back to playing baseball. The season opened late because of the strike. Frank had another great year at the plate. He hit 40 home runs with 111 runs batted in. He also hit a two-run homer in the All-Star Game. He was the first White Sox player ever to hit a home run in an All-Star Game.

But the White Sox didn't do as well in 1995. They dropped in the standings and missed out on postseason play.

His strength and discipline keep Frank hitting home runs.

Frank was determined to help the White Sox do better in 1996. He didn't waste any time. On the first pitch of his first at bat, Frank drove a home run to rightfield. With nine home runs and a .359 batting average by the end of April, Frank was named the American League Player of the Month.

He was chosen to be the starting first baseman in the All-Star Game. Frank had driven in 85 runs, an incredible total, by the All-Star break. But a few days before the big game, Frank hurt his foot in a game at Cleveland. He twisted his foot when he came to a quick stop after rounding first base. Frank stayed in the game and helped the White Sox win in extra innings, but the injury was serious. Tests revealed he had a stress fracture of the long bone in his left foot, from ankle to toe. He was placed on the disabled list and missed more than three weeks of the season, including the All-Star Game.

The White Sox missed Frank's big bat. They fell behind in the standings and never regained their momentum, even after Frank returned. Once again, they missed out on the playoffs. Frank still had a great season, though. He had clearly emerged as baseball's best hitter of the 1990s, as well as one of the best ever.

Frank finished second in the league with a .349 batting average and, despite the lost time because of the injury, hit 40 home runs. It was the sixth straight season in which he hit over .300 with 20 or more home runs and at least 100 walks, 100 runs scored, and 100 runs batted in. Only two players—Ted Williams and Lou Gehrig—had ever posted those numbers for as many as four years in a row.

Through it all, Frank's father in Columbus, Georgia, watches with pride. Frank bought his father a satellite television dish because Frank Sr. doesn't like to fly. Having missed out on a chance for a professional career himself, Frank Sr. lives his dream through his son. "When Frank is at bat," he says, "I feel like I'm at the plate. He's made me prouder than a father could be."

Career Highlights

Auburn University

Statistics

Year	Games	At bats	Runs	Hits	Doubles	Triples	Home runs	RBIs	Batting average
1987	59	209	56	75	12	0	21	68	.359
1988	55	182	45	70	21	0	9	54	.385
1989	64	206	62	83	19	3	19	83	.403
Totals	178	597	163	228	52	3	49	205	.382

Minor Leagues

Statistics

Year	Level	Team	Games	At bats	Runs	Hits	2B	3B	HR	RBIs	BB	Batting average
1989	Rookie	White Sox	17	52	8	19	5	0	1	11	10	.365
	Class A	Sarasota	55	188	27	52	9	1	4	30	31	.277
1990	Class AA	Birmingham	109	353	85	114	27	5	18	71	112	.323
Totals			181	593	120	185	41	6	23	112	153	.312

2B=doubles, 3B=triples, HR=home runs, BB=bases on balls (walks)

Honors

• *Baseball America's* choice as Minor League Player of the Year, 1990.

Major Leagues

Statistics

Year	Team	Games	At bats	Runs	Hits	2B	3B	HR	RBIs	BB	Batting average
1990	White Sox	60	191	39	63	11	3	7	31	44	.330
1991	White Sox	158	559	104	178	31	2	32	109	138	.318
1992	White Sox	160	573	108	185	46	2	24	115	122	.323
1993	White Sox	153	549	106	174	36	0	41	128	112	.317
1994	White Sox	113	399	106	141	34	1	38	101	109	.353
1995	White Sox	145	493	102	152	27	0	40	111	136	.308
1996	White Sox	141	527	110	184	26	0	40	134	109	.349
Totals		930	3,291	675	1,077	211	8	222	729	770	.327

2B=doubles, 3B=triples, HR=home runs, BB=bases on balls (walks)

Honors

• American League Most Valuable Player, 1993, 1994.
• *The Sporting News'* Major League Player of the Year, 1993.
• American League All-Star Team, 1993, 1994, 1995, 1996.*

Selected for the team but could not play because of an injury.

Glossary

at bat: An official attempt to hit a pitched ball. Hitting a sacrifice, being walked, or being hit by a pitch doesn't count as an at bat.

batting average: The number of hits a batter gets, divided by the batter's official at bats, carried to three decimal places. For example, if Frank gets 3 hits in 9 at bats, his batting average is .333.

chopper: A hard-hit ball that bounces in the infield.

count: The number of balls and strikes against a batter. The number of balls is always given first. For example, if the umpire has called two strikes on Frank but the pitcher has also thrown three balls to him, the count is 3-and-2—three balls and two strikes.

fielder's choice: A decision by a fielder who has fielded the ball to throw it to a base other than first base in order to put out a runner already on base. The batter isn't credited with a hit, even if the fielder doesn't get the other runner out.

grand slam: A home run hit with the bases loaded. A grand slam scores four runs.

run batted in (RBI): A run that is scored as a result of a batter getting a hit or, if the bases are loaded, the batter drawing a walk.

Frank has hit four grand slams for the White Sox.

scoring position: A baserunner on second or third base is said to be in scoring position because that runner might be able to score if the batter gets a hit.

twi-night doubleheader: Two games played one right after another, with the first game starting in the late afternoon and the second going on into the evening.

Index

ACKNOWLEDGMENTS

Photographs are reproduced with the permission of: pp. 1, 46, © John Klein; pp. 2, 35, 50, 52, 57, AP/Wide World Photos; pp. 6, 48, 58, © Mickey Pfleger/Sports California; p. 8, © ALLSPORT USA/Simon Bruty; p. 10, Archive Photos/Reuters/Brian Snyder; p. 13, © ALLSPORT USA/Doug Pensinger; pp.14, 18 (both), Seth Poppel Yearbook Archives; pp. 20, 23, 26, 29, Auburn University; p. 25, © ALLSPORT USA/Damian Strohmeyer; p. 30, Birmingham Barons/D. Weiss; pp. 39, 61, Sports-Chrome East/West; p. 40, © ALLSPORT USA/Jim Commentucci; p. 43, Archive Photos; p. 51, Archive Photos/Reuters/Moe Doiron; pp. 53, 63, © ALLSPORT USA/Jonathan Daniel; p. 55, © ALLSPORT USA/Jed Jacobsohn; p. 56, Archive Photos/Reuters/Scott Olson.

Front cover photograph by © Mickey Pfleger/Sports California Back cover photograph by AP/World Wide Photos. Artwork by John Erste.